EASY TO MAKE
NEEDLEPOINT

EASY TO MAKE NEEDLEPOINT

Stella Edwards
Series consultant: Eve Harlow

BROCKHAMPTON PRESS
LONDON

First published in Great Britain in 1991
by Anaya Publishers Ltd, Strode House,
44-50 Osnaburgh Street, London NW1 3ND

This edition published 1996 by Brockhampton Press,
a member of Hodder Headline PLC Group

Editor Eve Harlow
Design by Design 23
Photographer Di Lewis
Illustrator Kate Simunek
Charts Julie Ward

British Library Cataloguing in Publication Data

Edwards, Stella
Easy to make needlepoint. – (Easy to make)
I. Title II. Series
746.44
ISBN 1-86019-154-1

Typeset by Tradespools Limited, Frome, Somerset, UK
Colour reproduction by Columbia Offset, Singapore
Printed and bound in EC

CONTENTS

Introduction

For people of every age, needlepoint is a satisfying and rewarding occupation. Half cross stitch is mostly used and the techniques involved in working charted patterns are easy to understand.

Since early Saxon times women have applied needle and thread to decorate fabric. It was not until the 16th century, when metal needles were introduced, that the opportunity came to use fine wools, silks and gold threads. This greatly increased the variety of designs and types of embroidery and they have survived and continued to this day.

The term 'needlepoint' is often confused with 'tapestry'. Tapestry is, in fact, a woven fabric whereas needlepoint is the art of stitching a design on to a piece of canvas fabric. The confusion in terminology may have arisen because Victorian printed canvases for Berlin work often depicted scenes and themes derived from woven tapestries.

A wide range of items can be made using needlepoint and a number are featured in this book – cushions and footstools, bags and purses, bookmarks and pincushions. The basic stitch is half cross stitch and this is very easy to learn – it is demonstrated on this page. The only thing you have to remember is that all the stitches must lie in the same direction in a piece of work.

Tapisserie wool is mostly used in the projects, but in a few designs I have used stranded embroidery thread and gold thread. Occasionally, I have incorporated beads into my designs – just for a little sparkle.

Canvas is available from most needlework suppliers and comes in a fine mesh – 22 holes per inch – to a coarse mesh of 6 holes per inch. In this book I have limited myself to 12- and 10-hole canvas which as well as giving a reasonable amount of detail, also enables the work to 'grow' quite quickly.

Throughout this book, full colour charts are given for you to work the designs and you will find these very easy to follow. A key is given to help you to identify the wool colours and each square represents a half cross stitch.

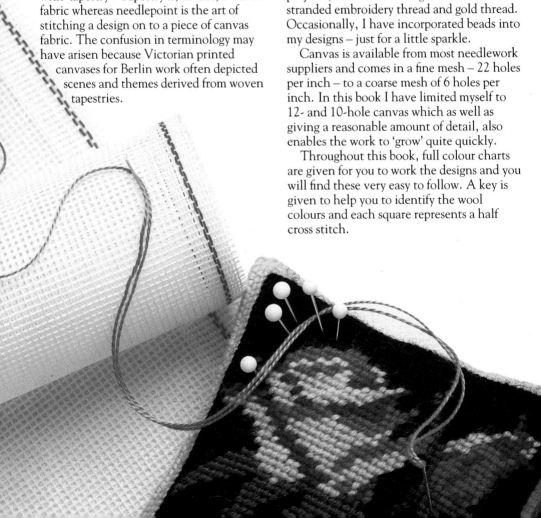

Some people like to use an embroidery frame for needlepoint. These help when large pieces are being worked, as a frame helps to prevent the canvas distorting during working. Most of my designs are small and you will be able to work holding the canvas in your hands. It is a good idea to bind the canvas edges with masking tape or to oversew them as this prevents the canvas from unravelling.

In any event, a light pressing on the back of the finished embroidery followed by a gentle pulling usually restores the canvas to shape.

I fell in love with needlepoint soon after I left university and I have been a passionate needlepointer ever since. I hope this book will make an enthusiast out of you also and that you will derive the same pleasure and satisfaction I have experienced from this relaxing and rewarding pastime.

Starting needlepoint
Cut wool from the skein to about 15in (37.5cm) – no longer – as it will wear thin as it is repeatedly pulled backwards and forwards through the canvas. Do not tie a knot in the end. Begin by passing the needle through the canvas from the top side, about 1in (2.5cm) from where you will begin embroidery, leaving a short tail hanging. Begin stitching. Pull the tail through after 3 or 4 stitches and work stitches over it. When the length of yarn is finished, darn the thread end under worked stitches.

Half cross stitch
This stitch can be worked from right to left or left to right, as you prefer. It is important that all the stitches slope in the same direction (Fig 1). Fig 2 shows the second row of stitches being worked. Fig 3 shows how your stitches should look on the wrong side of the work.

Fig 2

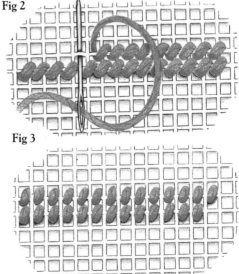

Fig 1

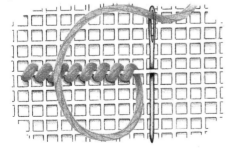

Fig 3

English rose

Pincushions, because they are small and quickly finished, are popular needlepoint projects. This one has a simple full-blown rose on the front and a bud motif on the back. For a more ornate effect, you could sew narrow, black guipure lace round the edges of the finished pincushion.

Materials
Piece of 12-hole interlock canvas 6 × 12in
(15 × 30cm)
Polyester toy stuffing
Anchor Tapisserie wool as follows: 1 skein
each of 386 pearl, 895 coral, 45 claret,
654 green and 3388 grass green; 2 skeins
of 23 pale pink; 3 skeins of 403 black

Preparation
1 Cut the canvas into two pieces 6in
(15cm) square. Mark the middle of both
pieces with vertical and horizontal lines of
basting stitches.

Working the embroidery
2 Follow the charts to work the design,
starting in the middle (indicated on the
edges with arrows). Use half cross stitch
throughout. The colours on the charts and
in the keys correspond with the wool colours
and numbers.

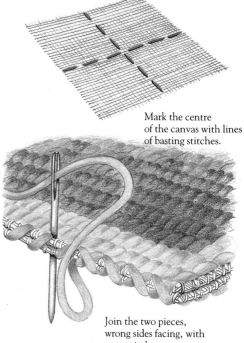

Mark the centre
of the canvas with lines
of basting stitches.

Join the two pieces,
wrong sides facing, with
cross stitch.

Chart 1

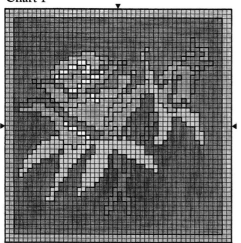

Chart 2

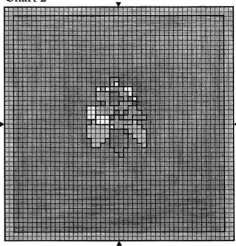

3 Work the front of the pincushion from chart 1 and the back from chart 2, working outwards from the motif to the edges and finishing with 2 rows of pink to match the front.

4 After completing both sides, press lightly on the back with a steam iron and gently pull the embroidery into shape. Trim canvas back to 4³/₄in (12cm) square.

Key

☐ 386	▨ 45
▨ 895	☐ 654
▨ 23	▨ 3388
	▨ 403

Finishing

5 Pincushions can be made up in two ways. In the first, place the two pieces together, right sides facing and machine-stitch or hand-sew on three sides. Trim corners diagonally, turn right sides out and stuff firmly. Turn in the canvas edges and slipstitch the seam to close.

6 The second method is worked from the right side of work. Fold the unworked canvas to the wrong side. Hold the front and back edges together, wrong sides facing. Work cross stitch over the edges (see illustration). Work on three sides of the pincushion, then stuff as stage 5. Close the fourth side with cross stitches.

11

Poppies and violets

Poppies and violets were popular flower motifs with Victorian embroideresses and this little pincushion has all the charm of that romantic period. This design is worked in rich, dark colourings but with a cream background a light, summery effect would be achieved.

Materials

Piece of 12-hole interlock canvas 6 × 12in (15 × 30cm)
Anchor Tapisserie wool as follows: 1 skein each of 634 cherry, 3388 grass green, 654 green and 620 hyacinth; 3 skeins of 403 black
Polyester toy filling

Preparation

1 Cut the canvas into two pieces 6in (15cm) square. Mark the middle of both pieces with vertical and horizontal lines of basting stitches (see page 10).

Working the embroidery

2 Follow the charts to work the design, starting in the middle (indicated on the edges of the charts with arrows). Use half cross stitch throughout. The colours on the charts and in the key correspond with the wool colours and numbers.

3 Work the front of the pincushion from chart 1 and the back from chart 2. Work outwards from the motif using the background colour, then finish the edges with 1 row of hyacinth to match the front.

4 After completing both sides, press lightly on the back with a steam iron and gently pull into shape.

Finishing

5 Make up the pincushion following one of the two methods described on page 10.

Chart 1

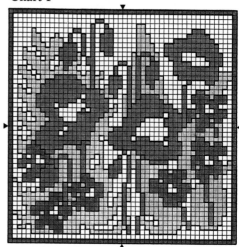

Chart 2

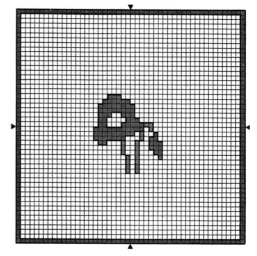

Key

☐ 403
▧ 634
▨ 3388
▤ 654
▦ 620

Green leaf

This simple design of a single leaf makes the needlecase an ideal project for a beginner – and what a pretty accessory for your work basket. An alternative colour scheme in red, green and white would make the needlecase an attractive and festive-looking Christmas gift. You might also sew pearl or glass beads to the leaf.

Materials

Piece of 12-hole interlock canvas 7 × 10in (17.5 × 25cm)

Anchor Tapisserie wool as follows: 1 skein each of 215 leaf green and 347 honey; 3 skeins of 729 ivory; small amount of 246 moss green

Lining fabric

Piece of white felt 4 × 7in (10 × 17.5cm)

Preparation

1 Cut the canvas into two pieces 7 × 5in (17.5 × 12.5cm). Mark the middle of both pieces with vertical and horizontal lines of basting stitches (see page 10).

Working the embroidery

2 Follow the chart to work the design, starting in the middle (indicated on the edges of the chart with arrows). Use half cross stitch throughout. The colours on the chart and in the key correspond with the wool colours and numbers.

3 Work both pieces of canvas with the design.

4 After completing the embroidery, press lightly on the back with a steam iron and gently pull into shape. Trim canvas back to within 12mm (¹/₂in) of embroidery. Cut lining to same size.

Finishing

5 Fold the unworked canvas to the wrong side on both pieces.

6 Hold back and front together wrong sides facing and join with cross stitches.

7 Press a hem to the wrong side all round the lining piece.

8 Hem the lining into the needlecase with tiny stitches and making sure that no unworked canvas shows.

9 Trim the felt with pinking shears, fold and sew inside the case, down the middle.

10 Left-over wools can be plaited together and tied round the case. Knot the plait ends into tassels.

Key

☐ 215
◪ 246
☐ 729
◼ 347

14

Ivy leaves and blossoms

A spectacle case with a design of ivy leaves and flowers makes an ideal gift and, with the addition of gold beads in the flower centres, the case looks even more luxurious.

Materials
Piece of 12-hole canvas 6 × 17in
 (15 × 43cm)
Anchor Tapisserie wool as follows: 1 skein
 each of 217 bottle green and 337
 apricot; 2 skeins of 215 leaf green; 4
 skeins of 340 auburn, 3¹/₂–4¹/₂yd
 (3–4m) of 336 rose
Gold beads
Lining fabric

Preparation
1 Cut the canvas in two pieces. Mark the middle of both with vertical and horizontal lines of basting stitches (see page 10).

2 Follow the chart to work the design on both pieces of canvas, starting in the middle (indicated on the edges of the chart with arrows). Use half cross stitch throughout.

3 After completing the embroidery, press lightly on the back with a steam iron and gently pull into shape. Sew gold beads in the middle of each flower.

Finishing
4 Trim both canvases back to within ¹/₂in (12mm) of embroidery. Cut the lining fabric to the same size.

5 On the embroidery, fold the excess canvas to the wrong side. Hold pieces together wrong sides facing and join the edges with cross stitch (see page 8).

6 Sew the two lining pieces together right sides facing, on three sides leaving the top edge open. Slip into the spectacles case.

7 Slipstitch the lining to the embroidery around the top edge.

8 For a decorative finish, some of the remaining wool can be plaited and sewn round the top edge.

Key
■ 337
■ 336
■ 217
□ 215
✗ 340

Pansy faces

This cheerful pansy picture would brighten any dull day and is simple enough for beginners to tackle. The design could be adapted for a pincushion or it would make a pretty cushion if worked on coarser canvas using cross stitch.

Materials

Piece of 10-hole double thread canvas 8in (20cm) square

Anchor Tapisserie wool as follows: 1 skein each of 727 buttercup, 634 cherry, 45 claret, 132 sapphire, 107 violet, 3150 jade, 3388 grass green and 403 black; 2 skeins of 729 ivory

Stiff backing card 6in (15cm) square

Preparation

1 Mark the middle of the canvas with vertical and horizontal lines of basting stitches (see page 10).

2 Follow the chart to work the design, starting in the middle (indicated on the edges of the chart with arrows). Use half cross stitch throughout. The colours on the chart and in the key correspond with the wool colours and numbers.

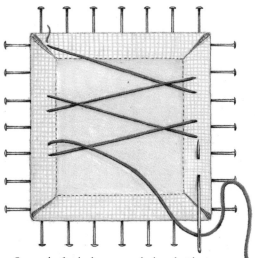

Secure the finished canvas to the board with pins pushed into the edges, stretching it smoothly and tightly as you work. Lace the canvas edges together with long stitches, side to side both ways.

3 When the embroidery is completed, press lightly on the back with a steam iron and gently pull into shape.

Finishing

4 To mount the embroidery for framing, spread over the card and pin the edges, pulling the surface of the canvas smoothly. Fold the unworked canvas over to the wrong side and lace together with button thread and long stitches.

Key

☐ 727			
▩ 107	▩ 634	▩ 45	▩ 132
▩ 403	☐ 3388	▩ 3150	☐ 729

Summer tints

This pretty pincushion would give the finishing touch to a bedroom – and, of course, it would make an ideal gift for a new bride. If you prefer, the cushion could be used as a sachet – just tuck a small bag of pot-pourri inside when stuffing it.

Materials
2 pieces of 12-hole interlock canvas 6 × 6in
(15cm) square
Anchor Tapisserie wool as follows: 2 skeins
of 23 pale pink, 1 skein of 118
cornflower and 3 skeins of 386 pearl
Polyester toy filling

Preparation
1 Mark the middle of the canvas with
vertical and horizontal basting stitches.

2 The charts shows the designs for the back
and front of the pincushion and the middles
are indicated on the edges with arrows.

Working the embroidery
3 Follow chart 1 to work the front of the
cushion (the colours and key correspond
with the wool colours and numbers). Work
chart 2 for the back of the cushion. Press the
embroidery lightly on the back and gently
pull into shape.

Finishing
4 Trim the canvas back to within ¹/₂in
(12mm) of the embroidery. Place the two
pieces of canvas together right sides facing
and stitch together on three sides. Trim the
corners diagonally, then turn to the right
side.

5 Stuff the pincushion with toy filling,
pushing it well into the corners.

6 Sew up the open side with slipstitches.
For a pretty finish, lace edging could be sewn
around the edges, gathering the lace as you
work. Allow twice the measurement all
round the pincushion for lace.

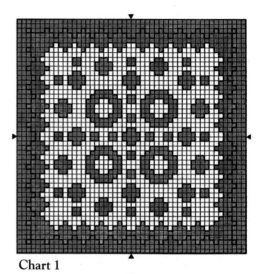

Chart 1

Key ☐ 386
      ▨ 23
      ◼ 118

Chart 2

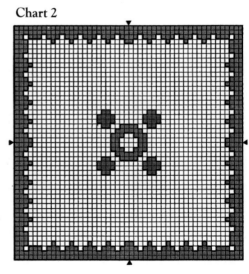

Bright poppies

Cheer up your breakfast table with poppies and sunshine colours. You might also make napkin rings to match, using the pattern on page 85.

Materials
For one eggcosy
Two pieces of 12-hole interlock canvas 6in (15cm) square
Anchor Tapisserie wool as follows: 3 skeins of 366 cream and a small amount of black 403;
Anchor Stranded cotton: 1 skein each of 46 red and 229 green
Lining fabric

Preparation
1 Mark the middle of both pieces of canvas with vertical and horizontal lines of basting stitches.

Working the design
2 Follow chart 1 for the front of the eggcosy and chart 2 for the back. The colours on the chart and in the key correspond with the wool and thread colours and numbers.

3 When the embroidery is completed, press lightly on the back with a steam iron and pull gently into shape.

4 Trim the unworked canvas back to within ³/₈in (9mm) of the embroidery.

Finishing
5 Use the embroidery to cut two pieces of lining fabric.

6 Place the two pieces of embroidery together, wrong sides facing and machine stitch round the curved edges, leaving the bottom open.

7 Turn right side out and press.

8 Make up the lining, stitching both pieces together, right sides facing.

9 Slip the lining into the eggcosy outer. Turn in the bottom edges and slipstitch together for a neat finish. For a finishing touch, sew plaited wool round the edges.

Chart 1

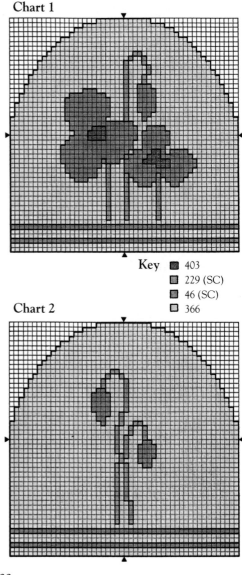

Key
■ 403
■ 229 (SC)
■ 46 (SC)
□ 366

Chart 2

TWO

Wildlife and Countryside

Jungle friends

Bright coloured macaws, and the luscious fruits and foliage of the South American rain forests make a brilliant picture for your home. The finished size is 15 × 9¹/₂in (38 × 24cm).

Materials
Piece of 10-hole double thread canvas size
    19 × 13in (48 × 34.5cm)
Anchor Tapisserie wool as follows: 1 skein
    each of 860 sage, 654 green, 3388 grass
    green, 729 ivory, 727 buttercup, 734
    daffodil, 3013 mustard, 628 chestnut,
    611 scarlet, 646 poppy, 635 crimson,
    386 pearl, 121 powder blue, 132
    sapphire, 148 deep blue, 707 navy and
    107 violet; 2 skeins of 218 malachite, 3
    skeins of 403 black
Stiff card for mounting the embroidery

Preparation
1 Mark the middle of the canvas with
vertical and horizontal lines of basting
stitches (see page 10).

Working the embroidery
2 Follow the charts on pages 28–29 to work
the design. The charts are broken across the
middle of the page and should be joined
where indicated with open arrows. The
middle of the design is indicated with black
arrows to correspond with your marked
canvas.

3 Use half cross stitch throughout. The
colours on the chart and in the key
correspond with the wool colours and
numbers.

4 After completing the embroidery, press
lightly with a steam iron on the back and
gently pull into shape. Cut the card to
15 × 9¹/₂in (38 × 24cm) and mount the
embroidery, lacing at the back, as described
on page 18.

5 The design would also make an unusual
cushion. Back it with velvet.

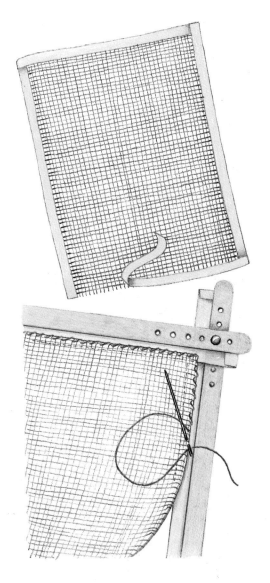

When working without a frame, cover the canvas edges
with masking tape to prevent fraying (top). Adjustable
frames can be adapted for small or large canvases. Sew
edges to the tapes (above).

Jungle friends charts

Join charts where indicated with open arrows. Black arrows indicate the middles of the charts.

Key
□ 860	□ 729	▨ 646	▨ 121	▨ 107
□ 654	□ 727	▨ 635	▨ 132	◙ 3013
▨ 3388	▨ 628	▨ 734	▨ 148	□ 403
▨ 218	▨ 611	▨ 386	▨ 707	

Mirror cats

Especially for cat lovers, this smart pair of felines makes an unusual design for a pincushion or can be framed for a small picture. The finished size of the design is 4¹/₂in (11.5cm) square but you could work it on a larger piece of canvas, adding a plain-coloured border.

Materials
Piece of 12-hole interlock canvas 6¹/₂ × 13in (16.5 × 33cm)
Anchor Tapisserie wool as follows: 1 skein each of 386 pearl, 399 grey and 403 black; 5 skeins 68 salmon and a short length of 144 pale blue grey
Polyester toy filling
Matching sewing thread

Preparation
1 Cut the canvas in two pieces and mark the middle of both pieces with vertical and horizontal lines of basting stitches (see page 10 for the technique).

Working the embroidery
2 Follow chart 1 to work the design for front starting in the middle (indicated on the chart edges with arrows). Use half cross stitch throughout. The colours on the chart and in the key correspond with wool colours and numbers.

3 Work the back of the pincushion from chart 2, working from the motif outwards until the back is the same size as the front.

4 After completing the embroidery, press lightly on the back with a steam iron and gently pull into shape. Trim excess canvas back to within ¹/₂in (12mm) of embroidery.

Finishing
5 Fold the unworked canvas to the wrong side all round. Right sides facing. Join front to back on three sides, using cross stitch (see page 10). Alternatively, join the pin cushion pieces right sides facing using machine- or hand-stitching. Then turn right side out.

6 Stuff the pincushion and close the open seam.

Key		
▢ 399		▦ 403
	▧ 144	▨ 68
		☐ 386

Chart 1   **Chart 2**

30

Butterfly box

Plastic canvas is just as easy to work on as the cotton type and has the added advantage that it is stiff enough to be able to be used for structures such as boxes.

Materials
Sheet of 7-hole plastic canvas
Anchor Tapisserie wool as follows: 1 skein each of 386 pearl, 872 lilac 105 lavender, 97 purple, 5 skeins of 895 coral and 9 skeins of 23 pale pink

Preparation
1 From the plastic canvas, cut 4 pieces 32 holes across and 33 holes down. From the remaining canvas, cut 1 piece 32 holes by 32 holes. In the middle of this piece cut a hole 10 holes by 12 holes (see note).

2 Work the top following chart 1. Follow chart 2 to work the butterfly design on the four side pieces. Use half cross stitch throughout and use the wool doubled in the needle. Follow the key for wool colours and numbers. Leave one plastic canvas thread unworked all round all four pieces. This will be used to join the pieces.

Finishing
3 Join the box sides using 895 coral, working in cross stitch, then add the top.

Note
It is important to centre the design on the canvas because it is very easy to begin in the wrong place. To prevent mistakes, cut the canvas with a few holes extra all round. Trim back to one hole all round for joining after embroidery is completed.

Ideas for the design
Use the butterfly motif to work a standing lamp base cover (see page 46), or the design would look pretty worked on a jewel box lid, with added beads.

Key ☐ 386   ▨ 105
      ▨ 895   ▨ 872
      ▨ 97   ☐ 23

Chart 1 **Chart 2**

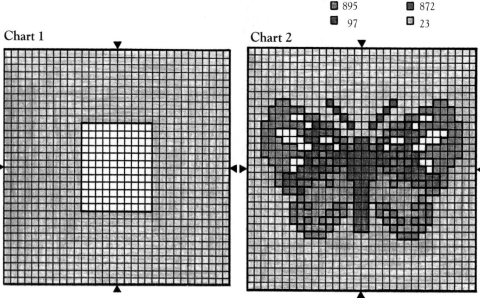

Hoppity bunny

Any little girl would be delighted with this tiny purse with its rabbit motif. Green and cream yarns are used here but the scheme could be varied to co-ordinate with a special outfit. You might also adapt the design for a matching pencil case.

Key

◨	570
▣	347
▨	617
▨	217
☐	386

Materials

Piece of 12-hole interlock canvas 8 × 4in (20.5 × 10cm)

Anchor Tapisserie wool as follows: 1 skein each of 347 honey and 570 magnolia, 3 skeins of 217 bottle green, small amounts of 386 pearl and 617 copper

Lining fabric

Two small press fasteners

Preparation

1 Mark the middle of the canvas with vertical and horizontal lines of basting stitches.

Working the embroidery

2 Follow the chart to work the design, starting in the middle (indicated on the edges of the chart with arrows). Use half cross stitch throughout. The colours on the chart and in the key correspond with the wool colours.

3 After completing the embroidery, press lightly on the back with a steam iron and gently pull into shape. Trim the canvas back to within 1/2in (12mm) of the embroidery.

4 Cut the lining fabric to the same size as the embroidery. Baste together right sides facing and machine stitch on three sides. Trim the corners diagonally and turn to the right side. Press and close the open seam with slipstitches.

5 Fold up the bottom third of the purse, so that a rabbit motif is on the flap. Wrong sides together, stitch the side seams of the purse together using cross stitch (see page 10). Sew on the press fasteners.

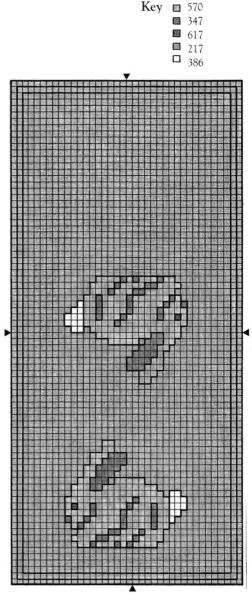

Bees and flowers

Matching accessories with a summery design of bright blooms and a busy bee to brighten any day. The charts for the pincushion and spectacles case are on the following pages.

PINCUSHION

Materials
Piece of 12-hole interlock canvas 6 × 12in (15 × 30cm)

Anchor Tapisserie wool as follows: 1 skein each of 625 dark green, 654 green, 895 coral, 646 poppy, 215 leaf green; 3 skeins of 665 straw; small amounts of 403 black, 734 daffodil, 3388 grass green

Polyester toy filling

Preparation
1 Cut the canvas into two pieces. Mark the middle of both with vertical and horizontal basting stitches (see page 10).

Working the embroidery
2 Follow chart 1 for the front of the pincushion and chart 2 for the back. Start in the middle of the charts (indicated on the edges with arrows).

3 Use half cross stitch throughout. The colours on the charts and in the key correspond with the wool colours and numbers.

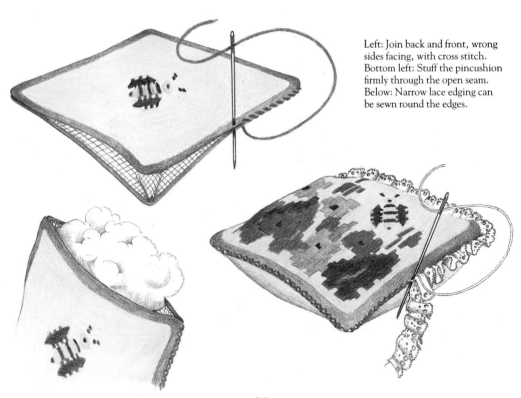

Left: Join back and front, wrong sides facing, with cross stitch.
Bottom left: Stuff the pincushion firmly through the open seam.
Below: Narrow lace edging can be sewn round the edges.

4 After completing the embroidery, press lightly on the back with a steam iron and gently pull into shape. Trim the canvas back to within ¹/₂in (12mm) of the embroidery.

5 Fold the unworked canvas to the wrong side on both pieces. Hold back and front together and join on three sides with cross stitches (see page 10). Stuff the cushion firmly and then close the open seam with cross stitches.

SPECTACLES CASE

Materials
Piece of 12-hole interlock canvas 6 × 17in (15 × 43cm)
Anchor Tapisserie wool as follows: 1 skein each of 734 daffodil, 895 coral, 646 poppy, 625 dark green, 654 green, 3388 grass green and 403 black; 2 skeins of 215 leaf green; 5 skeins of 665 straw
Lining fabric
Matching sewing thread

Preparation
1 Cut the canvas in two pieces. Mark the middle of both pieces with vertical and horizontal lines of basting stitches.

Chart 1

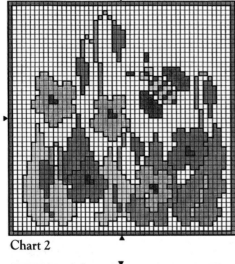

Chart 2

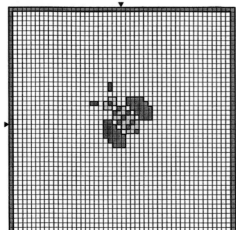

Key ☐ 665   ☐ 734
     ▨ 646   ▨ 625
     ▨ 895   ▨ 215
     ▨ 403   ☐ 654
     ◉ 3388

Chart 3

Working the embroidery

2 Follow chart 3 to work the design on both pieces of canvas. Start in the middle (indicated on the edges of the chart with arrows). Use half cross stitch throughout. The colours on the chart and in the key correspond with the wool colours and numbers.

3 After completing both pieces, press lightly on the back with a steam iron and gently pull into shape. Trim the excess canvas back to within ¹/₂in (12mm) of the embroidery. Cut two pieces of lining fabric to the same size as the embroidery.

Finishing

4 Fold the unworked canvas to the wrong side all round. Hold the case front and back together, wrong sides facing, and join the bottom and two side seams with cross stitch (see page 10).

5 Sew the two lining pieces together, right sides facing, on three sides and slip into the finished case. Turn in the top edges of both the embroidered outer and the lining and slipstitch together neatly.

Colouring lace
Antique-coloured lace looks effective on needlepoint items. If this cannot be obtained, soak a length of white lace in warm, strong tea to achieve a pinky brown colour.

THREE
Farmyard Friends
❧

Mother Goose

This small picture would be perfect for a child's room and is a good opportunity for you to practise new stitches on canvas. You could, if liked, work the design on coarse-mesh canvas to make a larger picture, or on 3-hole canvas for a cheerful bedroom rug.

Materials

Piece of 12-hole interlock canvas 7 × 5in (18 × 12.5cm)

Anchor Tapisserie wool as follows: 1 skein each of 386 pearl, 305 light yellow, 246 moss green, 634 cherry, 107 violet, 727 buttercup, 3149 apple green; 2 skeins of 654 green; three skeins of 505 grey green; small amount of 403 black

Stiff board for mounting

Preparation

1 Mark the middle of the canvas with stitches (see page 10).

Working the embroidery

2 Follow the chart to work the design, starting in the middle (indicated on the edges of the chart with arrows). Use half cross stitch as shown.

3 The fence and grass tufts are worked in straight stitches. Work the flowers in French knots.

4 When the embroidery is complete, press lightly on the back with a steam iron, pulling gently into shape.

Key

□	386	◨	654
◨	654	●	403
◨	634	□	505
□	107	◨	246
◨	3149		
◨	727		
□	305		

Finishing

5 Cut the mounting board to the area of the embroidery. Spread the embroidery over the board and pin into the board edges, pulling the canvas taut as you work.

6 Lace the canvas edges together on the back of the board, following the technique described on page 18.

Porky pig

This charming picture matches Mother Goose on page 42. French knots are used to provide additional texture.

Materials

Piece of 12-hole interlock canvas 7 × 5in (17.5 × 12.5cm)

Anchor Tapisserie wool as follows: 1 skein each of 121 powder blue, 3388 grass green, 868 shell pink, 386 pearl, 727 buttercup, 428 caramel, 347 honey, 337 apricot, 125 indigo, 734 daffodil, 381 chocolate, 634 cherry, 403 black, 399 grey, 3150 jade, 229 emerald, 654 green; a small amount of 611 scarlet

Stiff mounting board

Preparation

1 Mark the middle of the canvas with lines of basting stitches.

2 Following the chart work the design starting in the middle (indicated on the edges of the chart with arrows).

3 Use half cross stitch throughout except for the following: work the apples in four stitches of 634 cherry, then work a French knot in the centre using 611 scarlet.

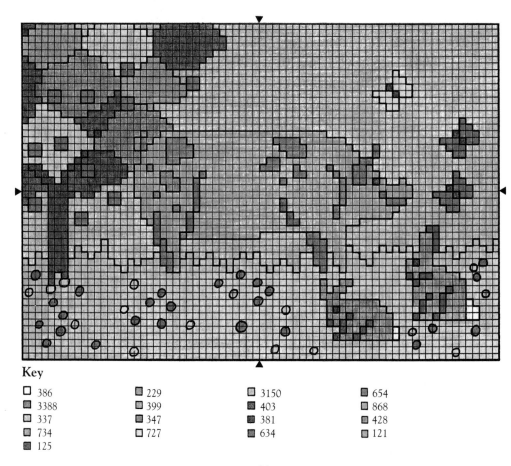

Key

☐ 386	▦ 229	☐ 3150	▦ 654
▦ 3388	☐ 399	▦ 403	☐ 868
☐ 337	▦ 347	▦ 381	▦ 428
☐ 734	☐ 727	▦ 634	▦ 121
▦ 125			

4 For the little flowers in the grass, stitch the background in 3388 grass green, then work in French knots, using varied colours.

5 When the embroidery is complete, press lightly on the back with a steam iron and pull gently into shape.

Finishing
6 Mount the picture as described for Mother Goose.

7 If preferred, both pictures could be glued, side by side, on a piece of cream-coloured board and framed together.

Goose and goslings

Make this little pincushion for a town friend to remind her of the country. The mother goose is on the front and three little goslings are on the back. The design could also be adapted for a needlecase.

Materials
Two pieces of 12-hole interlock canvas 6in (15cm) square
Anchor Tapisserie wool as follows: 1 skein each of 727 buttercup, 3025 marmalade, 339 blush pink, 639 verdure; 2 skeins of 3388 grass green, 386 pearl; 3 skeins of 744 damask pink; a small amount of 403 black
Polyester toy filling

Preparation
1 Mark the middle of both pieces of canvas with vertical and horizontal lines of basting stitches (see page 10).

Key
- ■ 403 (eye)
- □ 386
- ▨ 639
- □ 727
- ▨ 3025
- ▨ 339
- ▨ 744
- ▨ 3388

To make a cover for a lamp base, work the design on four pieces of plastic canvas, joining them with cross stitches.

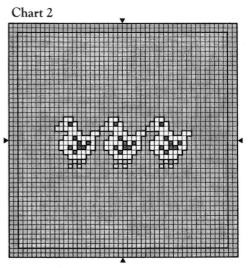

Chart 1

Chart 2

Working the embroidery

1 Follow chart 1 for the front of the pincushion, starting in the middle (indicated on the edges of the chart with arrows). Work the back of the pincushion from chart 2, working outwards from the motifs. Work two rows of 3388 grass green to finish the edges.

2 When the embroideries are complete press lightly on the back with a steam iron and gently pull into shape.

3 Fold the unworked canvas to the wrong side on both pieces and join with cross stitches (see page 10), leaving one side open.

6 Stuff the pincushion and close the fourth side with cross stitches.

FOUR

Fruit and Harvest

Fresh fruit

This bright picture of an apple and some cherries might make a picture for the kitchen. Alternatively, why not work it for a calendar heading? Enlarged, by working the design on a coarser canvas, the motif would make a charming cushion.

Materials
Piece of 10-hole canvas 8 × 8½in
 (20 × 21cm)
Anchor Tapisserie wools as follows: 1 skein
 each of 3236 olive, 280 lime green, 634
 cherry, 635 crimson, 625 dark green; 2
 skeins of 3013 mustard; 4 skeins of 729
 ivory; small amounts of 500 amber, 386
 pearl, 3072 plum, 381 chocolate
Piece of stiff board cut to the finished
 embroidery size

Preparation
1 Mark the middle of the canvas with
vertical and horizontal lines of basting
stitches (see page 10).

2 Follow the chart to work the design,
starting in the middle (indicated on the
edges of the chart with arrows). Use half
cross stitch throughout. The colours on the
chart and in the key correspond with the
wool colours and numbers.

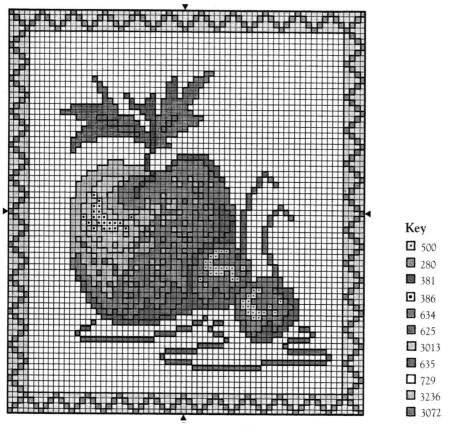

Key
- ⊡ 500
- ▦ 280
- ▨ 381
- ⊡ 386
- ▨ 634
- ▨ 625
- ☐ 3013
- ▪ 635
- ☐ 729
- ▨ 3236
- ▨ 3072

3 After completing the design, press lightly on the back with a steam iron and gently pull into shape.

4 Cut the card to size. Mount the canvas on the card by lacing the unworked canvas across the back (see page 18).

Sweet strawberries

This pretty sachet will provide a touch of summer wherever it is used. You might make several and display them in a small basket with green silk leaves around them, for an unusual accessory.

Materials
Two pieces of 12-hole interlock canvas
4 × 6in (10 × 15cm)
Anchor Tapisserie wool as follows: 1 skein each of 727 buttercup, 861 avocado, 634 cherry; 3 skeins of 386 pearl
Small muslin bag of pot-pourri
Polyester toy filling
Yellow ribbon for trimming

Preparation
1 Mark the middle of both pieces of canvas with vertical and horizontal lines of basting stitches (see page 10).

Working the embroidery
2 Follow the chart to work the design, starting in the middle (indicated on the edges of the chart with arrows). Use half cross stitch throughout. The colours on the chart and in the key correspond with the wool colours and numbers.

3 Work both pieces of the canvas with the design.

4 After completing the embroidery, press lightly on the back with a steam iron and gently pull into shape.

Finishing
5 Fold the unworked canvas to the wrong side on both pieces. Hold front and back together, wrong sides facing, and join on three sides with cross stitch (see page 10). Stuff, pushing in the pot-pourri bag. Close the open seam. Sew on a ribbon loop.

Repeat patterns
Needlepoint patterns, like this strawberry design, are ideal for working cushions because you can adapt the chart to cover any area you like. If the desired cushion, for instance, is 14in (35cm) square, you should cut the canvas at least 20in (50cm) square, mark out an area 15in (38cm) square and allow roughly 7–8 times more yarn than for the sachet.

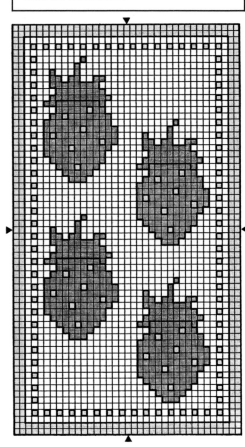

Key
☐ 727
▨ 861
▨ 634
☐ 386

Strawberries and trellis

This spectacles case is beautifully designed, with bright strawberries set into a trellis. For a special touch, glass beads are sewn on afterwards.

Materials
Piece of 12-hole interlock canvas 6 × 17 in (15 × 43 cm)
Anchor Tapisserie wools as follows: 1 skein each of 441 stone and, 727 buttercup; 3 skeins of 215 leaf green; 634 cherry; 4 skeins of 850 midnight blue
Lining fabric
Small yellow or gold beads

Preparation
1 Cut the canvas into two pieces. Mark the middle of both with vertical and horizontal lines of basting stitches (see page 10).

Working the embroidery
2 Follow the chart to work the design, starting in the middle (indicated on the edges of the chart with arrows). Use half cross stitch throughout. The colours on the chart and in the key correspond with the wool colours and numbers.

3 Work both pieces of canvas with the design.

4 After completing the embroidery, press lightly on the back with a steam iron and gently pull into shape. Trim the canvas back to within ½ in (12 mm) of the embroidery. Sew on the beads.

Finishing
5 Cut two pieces of lining fabric to the same size as the embroidery. Sew together on three sides leaving the top edge open.

Key ✗ Gold beads
□ 441
■ 634
□ 727
▨ 215
▦ 850

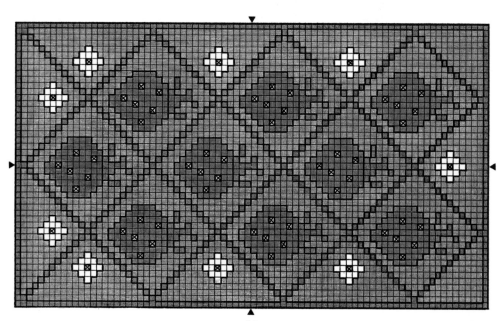

54

6 Fold the unworked canvas to the wrong side on both pieces of the embroidery. Hold the back and front together, wrong sides facing, and join the sides and bottom with cross stitches (see page 10).

7 Slip the lining into the case. Turn the top edges in and slipstitch together neatly.

55

Harvest home

Tissue box covers are useful accessories and this simple design can be worked in colours to suit any room scheme. The dimensions given will make a cover to fit an average-sized box of tissues.

Materials

One sheet of 7-hole plastic canvas.
Anchor Tapisserie wool as follows: 2 skeins of 428 caramel, 4 skeins of 726 sand; 10 skeins of 505 grey green

Preparation

1 Cut the canvas in pieces for the sides and top. Cut two sides 72 holes by 19 holes, two short ends 35 holes by 19 holes. Cut the top 72 holes by 35 holes. In the middle of the top, cut a hole 24 holes by 11 holes. (See note on page 32.)
2 Mark the middle of each piece with a thread or with a touch of felt-tipped pen.

Working the embroidery

3 Follow the charts to work the design, starting in the middle (indicated on the edges of the charts with arrows). Use half cross stitch throughout with doubled yarn in the needle. The colours on the charts and in the keys correspond with the wool colours and numbers. One hole is left unworked all round each piece for joining.

Finishing

4 Join pieces with cross stitch following the technique described on page 10. Work oversewing round the edges of the hole in the top and around the bottom edge.

Key

☐	726
▨	428
▦	505

Chart for ends

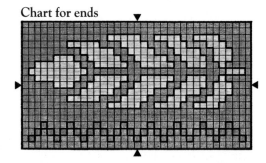

Chart for top

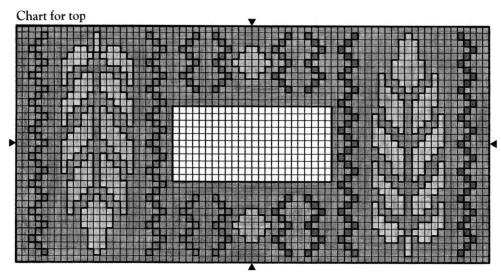

Chart for sides

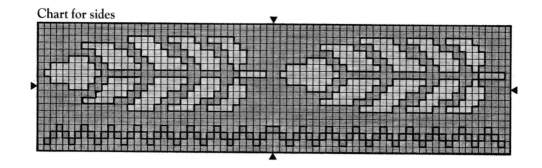

Bunches of grapes

Wooden boxes, similar to the one in the picture, can sometimes be obtained from needlework shops and suppliers (see page 96). The embroidery is mounted over the lid pad supplied and the finished result is extremely effective. The box shown here is for trinkets.

Materials

Piece of 12-hole interlock canvas 14 × 9in (35 × 23cm).

Anchor Tapisserie wool as follows: 1 skein each of 872 lilac, 125 indigo, 601 blue black, 3388 grass green, 2 skeins of 23 pale pink, 3 skeins of 386 pearl

Preparation

1 Mark the middle of the canvas with vertical and horizontal lines of basting stitches (see page 10).

2 The complete design is given in the chart and the middle of the design is indicated with arrows on the edges of the chart.

Working the embroidery

3 Start the embroidery in the middle of your canvas. Follow the chart and use half cross stitch throughout. The colours on the chart and in the key correspond with the wool colours and numbers.

4 When all embroidery is completed, press lightly on the back with a steam iron and gently pull into shape.

Finishing

5 Trim the canvas back to within ¹/₂in (12mm) of the embroidery.

6 Remove the pad from the box top. Pin the embroidery to the pad, making sure that

it aligns with the sides and ends. Stretch the canvas over to the back of the pad and lace the edges together (see page 18). Replace the lid on the box top.

Small pieces of needlepoint can be held in the hand for working, but canvases of this size, 14 × 9in (35 × 23cm) are easier to work in a frame.

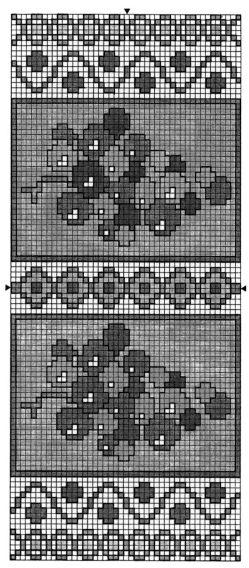

Key

▢ 23	▦ 872	▨ 125
▦ 3388	▢ 386	▦ 601

Adapting motifs

Motifs such as the grapes design can be abstracted for other needlepoint projects. Use the grapes motif alone for the cover of a note book or a cheque book cover (or perhaps, fittingly, for a wine diary). The end bands, being a formal repeat design, are ideal for working along a belt, either in single rows or several rows together. A single colour with metallic accents would look impressive.

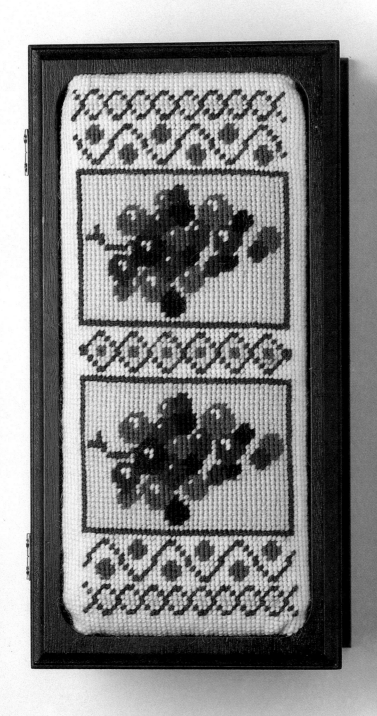

61

FIVE

Geometrics

Squares in squares

This striking cushion design is worked in squares of satin stitch over a varying number of threads. Four squares are set together to make a larger square and the embroidery is finished with backstitching.

Materials

Piece of 10-hole double thread canvas 16in (40cm) square

Anchor Tapisserie wool as follows: 2 skeins each of 45 claret, 707 navy; 3 skeins each of 132 sapphire, 229 emerald, 3199 ultramarine; 6 skeins of 403 black

16in (40cm) piece of velvet for backing
65in (162cm) of black dress braid
16in (40cm) cushion pad

Key ■ 45 ■ 3199 ■ 132
■ 707 □ 229 ■ 403

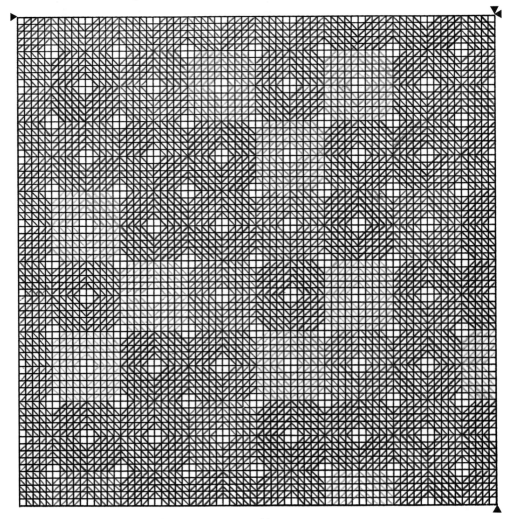

Preparation

1 Mark the middle of the canvas with vertical and horizontal lines of basting stitches (see page 10).

2 The top right quarter of the design is given on the opposite page and the middle of the design is indicated by arrows on the edges of the chart.

Working the embroidery

3 Begin in the middle of your marked canvas following the chart. The colours on the chart and in the key correspond with the wool colours and numbers. Work satin stitches over threads diagonally as shown.

4 When the first quarter has been worked, turn the chart and work the remaining three quarters of the design to match.

5 Finish by working backstitch between each colour block and through the centre of that block. This provides an interesting quilting effect and also ensures that the white canvas does not show through.

6 When the cushion cover has been completed, press the embroidery on the back with a steam iron and gently pull into shape.

7 Trim the canvas back to within ¹/₂in (12mm) of the embroidery.

Finishing

8 Place the embroidery and the velvet backing together right sides facing. Machine-stitch on three sides.

9 Trim the corners diagonally. Turn to the right side. Insert the cushion pad and slipstitch the open seam to close it.

10 To finish, you could sew a plait of yarn around the cushion edges, tying a loose knot at each corner.

Mark your place

Bookmarks are fun to make – the embroidery is completed in almost no time at all. These are decorated with motifs from Roman pottery and would make a thoughtful gift for both men and women.

Materials

Two pieces of plastic canvas 7-holes to 1in (2.5cm), 7¹/₂ × 1¹/₂in (19 × 4cm)
Anchor Tapisserie wool as follows: 1 skein each of 707 navy, 3199 ultramarine, 229 emerald and 97 purple
Tassels

Preparation

1 Each piece of canvas has an extra hole all round for finishing the edges.

2 Mark the middle of both strips of canvas, either with a thread or with a touch of felt-tipped pen.

Working the embroidery

3 Follow charts 1 and 2 for working the designs. The middle of the charts is indicated on the edges with arrows. Begin in the middle of your marked canvas. The colours on the charts and in the keys corresponds with the wool colours and numbers.

4 Use half cross stitch throughout and work with the yarn doubled in the needle.

5 Work neat oversewing stitches round the bookmarks.

6 Cut a piece of good quality fabric to the same size as the embroidery plus ¹/₂in (12mm) all round. Fold and press the fabric turnings to the wrong side.

7 Neatly hem the fabric lining to the back of the bookmarks.

8 For an elegant finish, sew a tassel to one end of each bookmark.

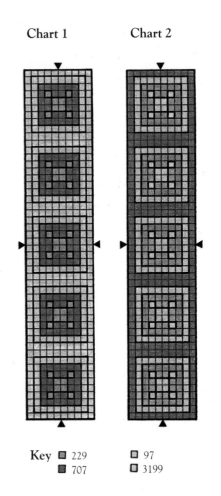

Chart 1   **Chart 2**

Key ☐ 229   ☐ 97
       ■ 707   ☐ 3199

Use the bookmark charts for working hairbands. Repeat the design to the desired length and mount the finished embroidery on velvet fabric. Sew elastic to the band ends to fit the head. You could also make matching wristbands from the same charts.

Prettily waisted

Needlepoint belts make smart fashion accessories and match most dress styles. The pattern given is a simple repeat motif so you can work the belt to any waist size you choose.

Materials

Piece of 10-hole double thread canvas 2in (5cm) wide and long enough to go round the waist plus 6in (15cm)

Anchor Tapisserie wool as follows: 1 skein each of 132 sapphire, 121 powder blue, 107 violet; 5 skeins of 403 black

(Note: The yarn quantities given are sufficient for up to 36in (90cm) waist. Allow extra yarn for longer belts.)

Dark blue beads

Cotton or chintz for lining

Buckle

Preparation

1 Mark the middle of your canvas with a thread or with a touch of felt-tipped pen.

2 Follow the chart to work the design, working from the middle of the repeat motif, indicated on the chart edges with arrows. Work towards the belt ends. Use half cross stitch throughout.

3 The colours on the chart and in the key correspond with the wool colours and numbers.

4 When the embroidery is completed, press lightly on the back using a steam iron and pull the canvas into shape, if there is any distortion.

5 Sew beads between the purple shapes following the picture on the opposite page.

6 Trim the canvas back to within 1/2in (12mm) of the embroidery.

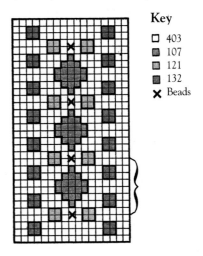

Key

☐ 403
■ 107
■ 121
■ 132
✕ Beads

Sew the buckle on to the belt end.

Sew the embroidery on to the lining.

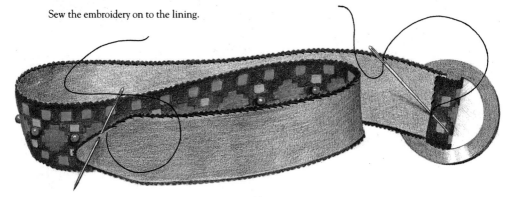

Finishing

7 Cut the lining fabric to the same size as the embroidery. Fold the unworked canvas to the wrong side all round the belt. Shape one end to a 'v'.

8 Press the turnings of the lining to the wrong side, shaping one end to a 'v'.

9 Place the embroidery and lining together, wrong sides facing, and neatly hem together. Slip the buckle on the end and sew in place.

After dark elegance

Luxurious and expensive-looking, needlepoint bags have a special cachet of their own. This one is worked in rich blues and purple but the colour scheme can be adapted to match any outfit. For instance, you might use a metallic thread instead of one of the colours – or even work the entire pattern in one basic shade.

Materials

Piece of 10-hole double thread canvas
  10 × 8in (25 × 20cm)
Anchor Tapisserie wool as follows: 1 skein
  each of 132 sapphire and 121 powder
  blue; 2 skeins 107 violet; 3 skeins 403
  black
Dark blue and silver beads
Piece of black velvet 26 × 10in
  (66 × 25.5cm)
Two decorative motifs (optional)
Ribbon for handle

Preparation

1 Mark the middle of the canvas with vertical and horizontal lines of basting stitches.

Working the embroidery

2 Follow the chart to work the design, starting in the middle (indicated on the edges with arrows). Use half cross stitch throughout. The small circles and crosses indicate positions of beads.

Key □ 403   ▣ 132   ▦ 121
        ▩ 107   ✗ Blue beads   O Silver beads

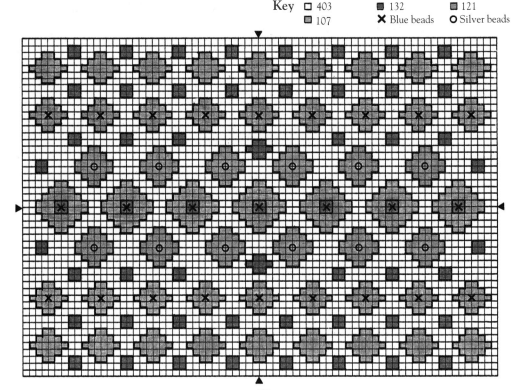

3 The colours on the chart and in the key correspond with wool colours and numbers.

4 When the embroidery is completed, press lightly on the back with a steam iron and gently pull into shape.

5 Sew on the beads, following the picture.

Making up the bag

6 Spread the velvet pile side down and fold the short ends to meet in the middle. Sew together with oversewing, catching both layers of velvet in the stitches.

7 Turn the piece of velvet over, fold, and machine-stitch the sides of the bag.

8 Turn right side out.

9 Trim the unworked canvas back to within $^{1}/_{2}$in (12mm) of the embroidery. Fold the canvas to the wrong side. (Fold right up to the stitches so that no canvas shows on the edges.)

10 Catch the embroidery to the bag front. Sew on the ribbon handle. Sew the motifs over the ends.

Greet the sun

If you are just a beginner, you'll enjoy making a case for sunglasses.
Work just one side and back the piece with fabric, or work two sides.
Either way, you'll have a piece of needlepoint to be proud of.

Materials
Piece of 12-hole interlock canvas 4 × 6½in (10 × 16.5cm)
Anchor Tapisserie wool as follows: 1 skein each of 646 poppy, 3025 marmalade, 625 dark green, 381 chocolate; 2 skeins of 850 midnight blue
Backing fabric
Lining fabric

Preparation
1 Mark the middle of the canvas with vertical and horizontal lines of basting stitches.

Working the embroidery
2 Follow the chart to work the design, starting in the middle (indicated on the edges with arrows). Use half cross stitch

throughout. The colours on the charts and in the key correspond with wool colours and numbers.

3 Follow the picture to repeat the design to complete the embroidery.

4 After completing the embroidery, press lightly on the back with a steam iron and gently pull into shape. Trim the canvas back to ½in (12mm) from the embroidery.

Finishing
5 Use the embroidery to cut a matching shape from the backing fabric.

Key
646
3025
625
850
381

6 Using the embroidery, cut two pieces from the lining fabric.

7 Place the embroidery and backing together, right sides facing. Machine-stitch all round, leaving the top edge open.

8 Trim back the seam allowance and cut the corners off diagonally. Turn the case to the right side and press lightly on both sides.

9 Stitch the lining pieces together right sides facing. Trim the seam allowance and slip into the case.

10 Turn in the top edges and slipstitch the lining to the case around the top edge.

11 To trim the case you could plait the remaining yarns together and sew the plait round the case edges.

Sparkler

Designed for very special occasions, you'll look and feel your best with this beautiful accessory in needlepoint. The pattern can be adapted to other colour schemes and the beads can be omitted if desired.

Materials
Piece of 12-hole interlock canvas 10 × 5in (25.5 × 12.5cm)
Anchor Tapisserie wool as follows: 1 skein each of 701 russet, 654 green, 729 ivory; 4 skeins of 3055 mahogany
Gold beads
Lining fabric
2 press fasteners

Preparation
1 Mark the middle of the canvas with vertical and horizontal lines of basting stitches.

Working the embroidery
2 Follow the chart on page 76 to work the design, starting in the middle (indicated on the edges with arrows). Use half cross stitch throughout. The colours on the charts and in the keys correspond with the wool colours and numbers.

3 After completing the embroidery, press lightly on the back with a steam iron and gently pull into shape.

4 Sew gold beads to the middle of each flower.

5 Trim the canvas back to within ¹/₂in (12mm) of the embroidery. Use the embroidery to cut the same shape from lining fabric.

6 Fold the unworked canvas to the wrong side. Press the seam allowance of the backing fabric to the wrong side.

7 Sew the backing to the embroidery using small hemming stitches, making sure that the canvas edges are covered.

Hem the backing to the embroidery.

Then join the purse sides.

Sew press fasteners to secure the purse.

74

8 Fold the purse and join the edges using cross stitch (refer to page 10). Sew the press fasteners to the purse and to the underside of the flap.

9 If a carrying strap is required, machine-stitch two lengths of satin ribbon together, wrong sides facing, along the edges, sew ends to the inside of the bag, under the flap.

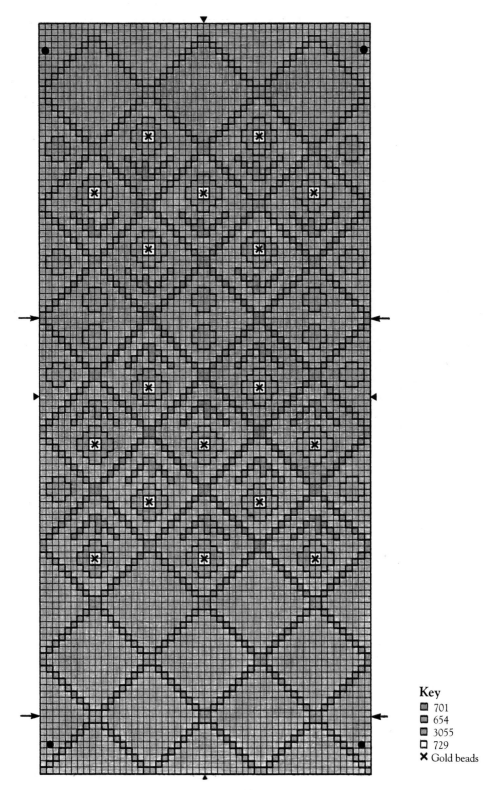

Key

- 701
- 654
- 3055
- 729
- ✗ Gold beads

Deal the cards

This smart card box would make an ideal gift for card-playing friends. The four suits are used as decorative motifs but you could work the pattern pieces without the motifs if you prefer.

Materials
Sheet of 7-hole plastic canvas
Anchor Tapisserie wool as follows: 3 skeins
    each of 634 cherry and, 229 emerald;
    12 skeins of 707 navy
Fabric for lining

Preparation
1 Cut the plastic canvas for the box top,
bottom and sides as follows: cut 1 top 34
holes by 53 holes plus one extra hole all
round for joining. Cut the bottom to the
same size. Cut two sides 53 holes by 16
holes, cut two ends 34 holes by 16 holes, all
with an extra hole all round for joining.
(See note on page 32.)

Working the embroidery
2 Mark the middle of the canvas pieces with
a thread, or with a touch of felt-tipped pen.

77

Bottom (1)

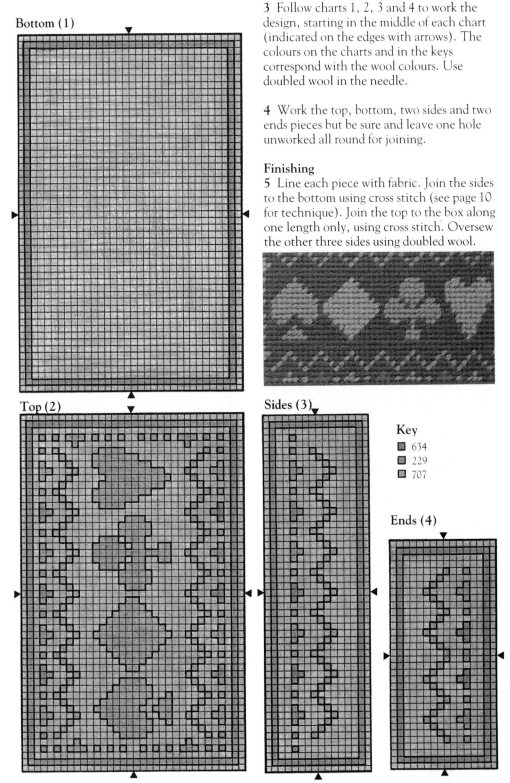

3 Follow charts 1, 2, 3 and 4 to work the design, starting in the middle of each chart (indicated on the edges with arrows). The colours on the charts and in the keys correspond with the wool colours. Use doubled wool in the needle.

4 Work the top, bottom, two sides and two ends pieces but be sure and leave one hole unworked all round for joining.

Finishing

5 Line each piece with fabric. Join the sides to the bottom using cross stitch (see page 10 for technique). Join the top to the box along one length only, using cross stitch. Oversew the other three sides using doubled wool.

Top (2)

Sides (3)

Key
■ 634
■ 229
■ 707

Ends (4)

Flowers and diamonds

Needlework footstools are always greatly admired, and will be treasured for years to come. This design is one that can be adapted to any size stool, or you could work it on a chair seat. It also makes an ideal all-over pattern for a cushion (see page 82).

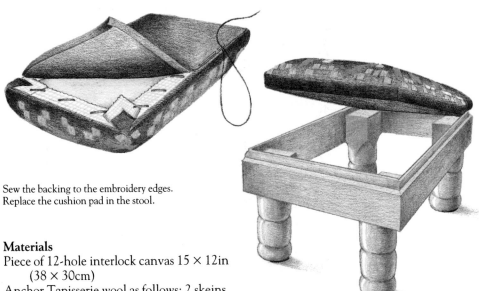

Sew the backing to the embroidery edges.
Replace the cushion pad in the stool.

Materials
Piece of 12-hole interlock canvas 15 × 12in
(38 × 30cm)
Anchor Tapisserie wool as follows: 2 skeins
each of 895 coral, 872 lilac, 897 garnet,
3199 ultramarine and 3149 apple green;
3 skeins each of 3388 grass green and
229 emerald; 9 skeins of 403 black
Backing fabric

Preparation
1 Half of the design is given in the chart on
page 81 and the middle is indicated with
black arrows on the edges. Work the other
half of the stool top to match.

2 Mark the middle of the canvas with
vertical and horizontal lines of basting
stitches.

Working the embroidery
3 Follow the chart to work the design
starting in the middle of your canvas. Use
half cross stitch throughout.

5 Press the finished embroidery lightly on
the back with a steam iron and pull gently
into shape.

Finishing
6 Spread the embroidery over the cushion
pad and pull over to the underside. Staple
the embroidery to the wood frame, folding
the corners.

7 Cut the backing to shape, turn under the
edges, sew the backing to the embroidery.

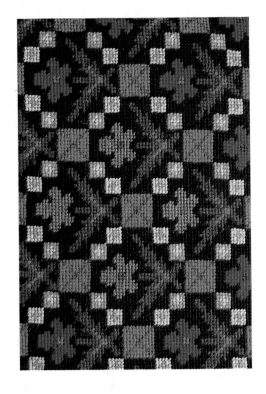

The cushion on page 82 is worked from the chart
opposite using the alternative colour scheme.

Key
- 872 (337)
- 897 (617)
- 895 (105)
- 3199 (107)
- 3388 (147)
- 3149 (336)
- 229 (508)
- 403 (386)

Colours in brackets are for the cushion on page 82.

Made for each other

This cushion uses the same chart as the stool on page 80 but the colour scheme is different and the canvas is 10-hole. If you prefer, make the cushion and stool to match for a pair of pretty room accessories. The cushion can be made to any size (see stage 1), and can have embroidery on both sides.

Materials
Piece of 10-hole canvas 20in (50cm) square
Anchor Tapisserie wool as follows: 1 skein
  each of 107 violet and 337 apricot; 2
  skeins each of 508 bluebell, 105
  lavender, 336 old rose and 617 copper;
  3 skeins each of 147 azure; 10 skeins of
  386 pearl
Piece of backing velvet 16in (40cm) square
16in (40cm) cushion pad

Preparation
1 Mark the middle of the canvas with vertical and horizontal lines of basting stitches. Begin in the middle of the stool chart and work outwards until you have a piece of embroidery 16in (40cm) square.

Working the embroidery
2 Follow the chart on page 80 but using the key for the cushion to work the embroidery in half cross stitch.

3 Press the finished embroidery lightly on the back with a steam iron and pull gently into shape.

Making cushions
Needlepoint cushions look better with a decorative cord sewn around the edges, or you can make a thick plait of leftover wool. Four colours look best; plait together three mixed bunches of about 9 strands each, enough to go round the cushion. At one corner, knot the plaits and cut the ends short to make a double tassel.

Soft jewellery
Motifs from needlepoint designs can be adapted to make soft jewellery. Plastic or regular canvas can be used. Work designs in wool, doubled stranded cotton, metallic or chenille threads. Decorate embroidery with glass or metallic beads, diamanté or glass ornaments, etc. Turn the edges of the finished embroidery and sew to velvet, padding behind the worked piece with tufts of polyester wadding. Use this method to work pendants, earrings, bracelets and hairbands for evening wear. Soft needlepoint jewellery looks particularly effective when worked in shades of yellow with gold thread, with a single contrasting colour.

Finishing
4 Trim the unworked canvas back to $\frac{1}{2}$in (12mm) from the embroidery.

5 Place the embroidery and velvet backing together, right sides facing, and stitch on three sides. Insert the cushion pad and close the fourth side with slipstitches.

6 A plait of wool can be sewn around the cushion edges to give it a professional-looking finish. Use the colours 107, 337, 105 and 336. You will need to allow an extra skein of each colour to make a plait.

Fine service

Pretty napkin rings add a touch of elegance to any table – and take very little time to work. This design is in the same colour scheme as the poppies eggcosy on page 22 and might therefore be made as a matching breakfast set for a special gift.

Materials
(To make one ring)
Piece of 12-hole interlock canvas 7 × 3in (18 × 7.5cm)
Anchor Stranded cotton as follows: 1 skein each of 46 red and 229 green;
Anchor Tapisserie wool as follows: 1 skein of 366 cream
Lining fabric

Preparation
1 Mark the middle of the canvas with vertical and horizontal basting stitches.

Working the embroidery
2 Follow the chart to work the design, starting in the middle (indicated on the edges with arrows). Use half cross stitch throughout. The colours on the chart and in the key correspond with the colours and numbers.

3 When the embroidery is completed, press lightly on the back with a steam iron and pull gently into shape.

Finishing
4 Trim the canvas back to within ¼in (6mm) of the embroidery. Trim the canvas corners diagonally. Cut the lining fabric to the same size.

5 Fold the unworked canvas to the wrong side. Press the edges of the lining fabric to the wrong side.

6 Put the embroidery and lining together, wrong sides facing and sew the edges together, making sure no canvas shows on the edges.

7 Join the napkin ring ends together with oversewing, hemming or cross stitch.

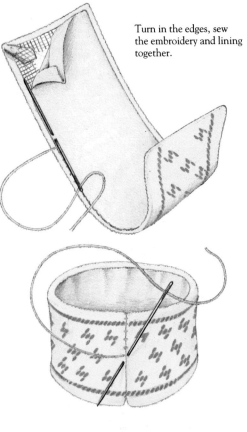

Turn in the edges, sew the embroidery and lining together.

Join the ends with small, neat stitches.

Key
■ 46 (SC)
■ 229 (SC)
□ 366

84

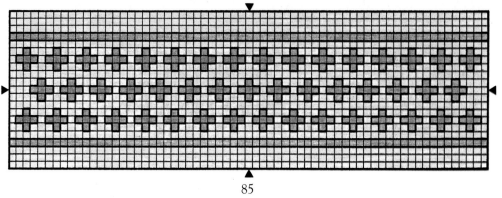

SIX

Special Occasions

Brides' delight

Sachets like this make ideal wedding gifts and will be treasured for years to come. The heart shape could be given an individual touch by working it as a pincushion. Spear small pearl beads on pins and outline some of the design for a different effect.

HEART SACHET

Materials
Two pieces of 12-hole interlock canvas 5in (12.5cm) square
Anchor Stranded cotton as follows: 1 skein each of 74 pink and 128 blue
Anchor Tapisserie wool: 1 skein each of 144 blue-grey and 23 pale pink
Polyester toy filling
Lavender bag

Preparation
1 Mark the middle of both pieces of canvas with vertical and horizontal basting stitches.

Working the embroidery
2 Follow the chart to work the design starting in the middle (indicated on the edges of the chart with arrows). Use half cross stitch throughout. Work one piece of canvas with the design in blue-grey stranded cotton on a pink wool ground and the other with the design in pink stranded cotton on a blue-grey wool ground.

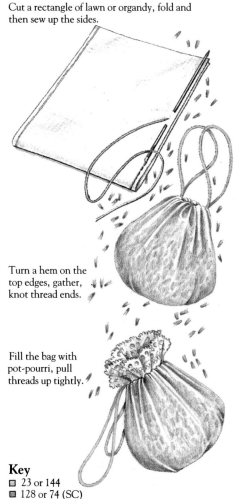

Cut a rectangle of lawn or organdy, fold and then sew up the sides.

Turn a hem on the top edges, gather, knot thread ends.

Fill the bag with pot-pourri, pull threads up tightly.

Key
☐ 23 or 144
▨ 128 or 74 (SC)

3 When both pieces of canvas have been worked, press lightly on the back with a steam iron and pull gently into shape.

4 Trim the canvas back to within ¹/₂in (12mm) of the embroidery.

Finishing

5 Sew both heart shapes together, right sides facing, leaving a gap for filling. (If preferred, sew the hearts together with cross stitches, using the technique described on page 10).

6 Turn to the right side and stuff the heart sachet with toy filling, pushing in a small bag of dried lavender. Close the open seam with slip stitches.

SQUARE SACHET

Materials
Piece of 12-hole interlock canvas 7in
    (18cm) square
Anchor Tapisserie wool as follows: 1 skein of
    868 shell pink; 2 skeins each of 386
    pearl and 729 ivory
Anchor Stranded cotton as follows: 2 skeins
    of white
Piece of velvet for backing
Small pearl beads
Small bag of dried lavender
Polyester toy filling

Preparation
1 Mark the middle of the canvas with
vertical and horizontal lines of basting
stitches.

Working the embroidery
2 Follow the chart to work the design,
starting in the middle (indicated on the
edges of the chart with arrows). Use the
stitches, wools, threads and colours as
indicated in the key.

3 When the embroidery is completed, press
lightly on the back with a steam iron and
gently pull into shape.

Finishing
4 Sew the beads to the embroidery as shown
on the chart.

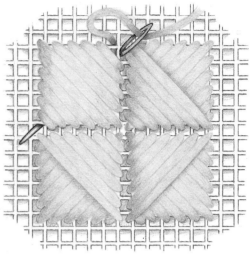

Cross-cornered cross stitch
A square is worked in diagonal stitches, then the
square is covered with diagonal stitches worked the
other way. Four squares make the complete cross-
cornered cushion stitch.

5 Trim the canvas back to within ¹/₂in
(12mm) of the embroidery. Use the
embroidery to cut the backing from velvet
fabric.

6 Place the embroidery and backing
together, right sides facing, and stitch on
three sides and part of the fourth.

7 Turn right side and stuff with toy filling,
pushing in the lavender bag. Close the open
seam with slip stitches.

90

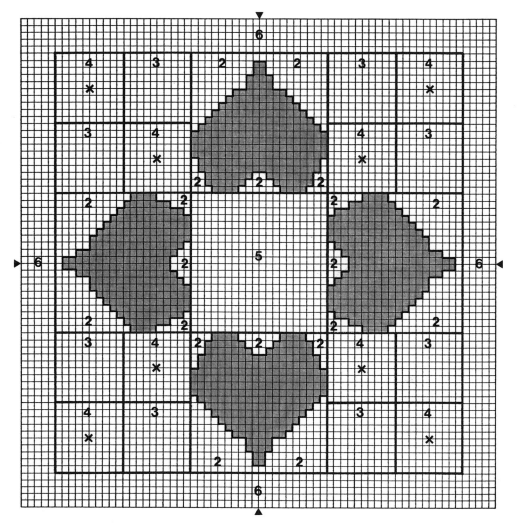

Key

1 Half cross stitch in 868

2 Half cross stitch in 386

3 Half cross stitch in white SC

4 Cross-cornered cushion stitch in 729

5 Rice stitch in 386 then white SC

6 Rice stitch in 729 then 386

x Small pearl beads

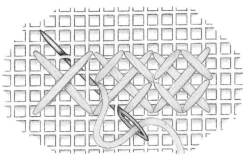

Rice stitch
Work a cross stitch first, then work a straight stitch diagonally over each of the arms.

Christmas fun

Three festive pictures to decorate your home at Christmas – or you might work them as very special greetings cards. The designs are also adapted to make small tree decorations.

PICTURES

Materials

Three pieces of plastic 7-hole canvas 27
    holes × 46 holes
Felt for lining
Ribbon for hangers
Anchor Tapisserie wool as follows:

Snowman

1 skein each of 634 cherry, 727 buttercup,
    403 black and 132 sapphire, 2 skeins
    each of 386 pearl

Cracker

2 skeins each of 229 emerald, 634 cherry; 1
    skein each of 727 buttercup and 386
    pearl
Scrap of narrow ribbon

Christmas tree

2 skeins of 229 emerald, 3 skeins of 386
    pearl, 1 skein each of 132 sapphire and
    634 cherry
Gold beads
Gold embroidery thread

Preparation

1 Mark the middle of each piece of canvas
with a touch of felt-tipped pen.

Working the embroidery

2 Follow the charts to work the designs
starting in the middle (indicated on the
edges of the charts with arrows). Use half
cross stitch throughout, with wool doubled
in the needle.

3 Sew ribbon scrap across the middle of the
cracker. Sew on beads. Embroider a star as
shown using gold thread.

Finishing

4 Oversew the edges of the finished
embroideries to neaten, using doubled wool.
Cut felt to the same size as the pictures.
Hem to the back, using matching sewing
thread.

5 Sew hangers to the backs of the pictures.

Using the motifs
If four pieces of plastic canvas are
worked with the design, a four-sided
Christmas tree ornament can be
constructed. Sew together on the sides,
then tie hanging threads to the top
corners.

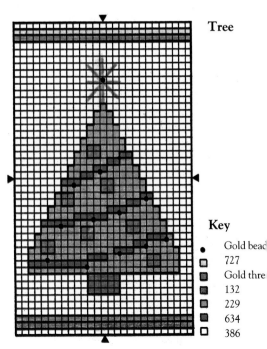

Tree

Key

●	Gold bead
▫	727
▪	Gold thread
▪	132
▪	229
▪	634
▫	386

Cracker

Snowman

Key
- ▨ 229
- ☐ 727
- ▨ 634
- ◉ Gold thread
- ☐ 386

Key
- ▨ 634
- ☐ 727
- ▨ 403
- ▨ 132
- ☐ 386

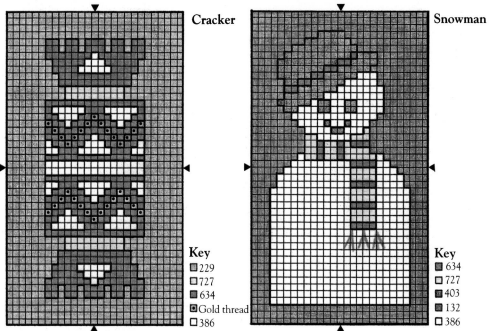

TREE ORNAMENTS

Materials
Six pieces of plastic 7-hole canvas 11 holes
× 9 holes
Anchor Tapisserie wool as follows: small
    quantities of 611 scarlet, 403 black,
    727 buttercup; 1 skein each of 132
    sapphire, 386 pearl and 229 emerald
Gold beads, gold thread

Preparatrion
1 Mark the middle of each piece of canvas
with a touch of felt tipped pen.

Working the embroidery
2 Follow the charts to work the designs,
starting in the middle (indicated on the
edges of the charts with arrows). Use half
cross stitch throughout with wool doubled in
the needle.

3 Work two of each design, one for the
front of the ornament and one for the back.

4 Stitch the front and back together with
oversewing using the same yarn colour as
used for the background.

5 Decorate with gold beads and threads (see
picture).

6 Thread a length of yarn on to needle, pass
through the top of each ornament for a
hanger.

Gift tags
Tree ornaments can also be used to
make unusual gift tags. Work the design
once for each tag, oversew the edges
with wool then mount the ornament on
to good quality coloured paper. Write
your message and tie the ornament to
the gift with narrow gold ribbon.

Use the Christmas motifs for
greetings cards. Glue the embroidery
into card blanks then fold the
card and glue behind
the embroidery.

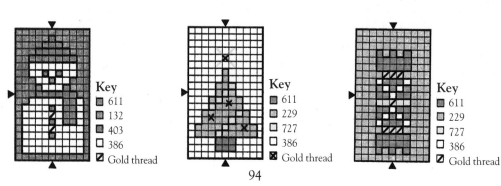

Key
- 611
- 132
- 403
- 386
- Gold thread

Key
- 611
- 229
- 727
- 386
- Gold thread

Key
- 611
- 229
- 727
- 386
- Gold thread

Acknowledgements and Source List

Anchor Tapisserie Wool and Stranded Cotton supplied by
Coats Patons Crafts,
P.O. Box, McMullen Road,
Darlington,
Co. Durham DL1 1YQ, UK.

Trinket box from Harper Holland Ltd,
11–12 Industrial Park, Harbour Road Rye,
East Sussex TN31 7TS, UK.

Footstool from Casa Needlepoint (address below).

All the designs in this book are by the author.

Author Stella Edwards' needlepoint kits are available
internationally by mail order from:

Casa Needlepoint,
39 Merton Avenue,
Chiswick,
London W4 1TA, UK